The Faith Topical Bible

John Eckhardt

More materials available at

John Eckhardt Ministries.com

Table of Contents

Introduction

The large number of references in Scripture reveal the importance of faith in the believer's life. Faith is connected to the word of God, and faith comes by hearing. Without faith it is impossible to please God. In other words, faith pleases God. We are called to live by faith. Faith affects every area of one's life. ThisTopical Bible contains every scripture in the bible concerning faith. It will be a handy reference tool for believers who desire to grow in their faith.

The Greek word for FAITH is **PISTIS** meaning faith, belief, trust, confidence; fidelity, faithfulness.

The Hebrew word for FAITH is **AMANAH** meaning agreement, firm regulation, in other words, it is agreeing with God and his word, saying Amen.

Amen means "to lean on for support." It is usually translated "believe." It is used of the faith for salvation and pictures someone leaning on God (Genesis 15:6).

YAQAL (Job 13:15) means "to trust in extreme pain; to trust under pressure." It is usually translated "hope."

QAWAH, the strongest Hebrew word for faith, is translated "wait."

Unbelief and doubt will hinder a person from receiving the promises of God. Fear is another enemy of faith, and will hinder one from receiving.

Key Scriptures for this Topical Bible:

Hebrews 11:6

"But without **faith** it is impossible to please him: for he that cometh to God must believe that he is, and that he is a rewarder of them that diligently seek him,"

2 Thessalonians 1:3

"We are bound to thank God always for you, brethren, as it is meet, because that your **faith** groweth **exceedingly**, and the charity of every one of you all toward each other aboundeth," and Romans 10:17, "So then **faith** cometh by **hearing**, and **hearing** by the word of God."

The Book of Genesis

Genesis 15:6
And he **believe**d in the Lord; and he counted it to him for righteousness.

The Book of Exodus

Exodus 4:4-6
And the Lord said unto Moses, Put forth thine hand, and take it by the tail. And he put forth his hand, and caught it, and it became a rod in his hand:
That they may **believe** that the·Lord God of their fathers, the God of Abraham, the God of Isaac, and the God of Jacob, hath appeared unto thee. And the Lord said furthermore unto him, Put now thine hand into thy bosom. And he put his hand into his bosom: and when he took it out, behold, his hand was leprous as snow.

Exodus 4:8
And it shall come to pass, if they will not **believe** thee, neither hearken to the voice of the first sign, that they will **believe** the voice of the latter sign.

Exodus 4:9
And it shall come to pass, if they will not **believe** also these two signs, neither hearken unto thy voice, that thou shalt take of the water of the river, and pour it upon the dry land: and the water which thou takest out of the river shall become blood upon the dry land.

Exodus 4:31
And the people **believed**: and when they heard that the Lord had visited the children of Israel, and that he had looked upon their affliction, then they bowed their heads and worshipped.

Exodus 19:9
And the Lord said unto Moses, Lo, I come unto thee in a thick cloud, that the people may hear when I speak with thee, and **believe** thee for ever. And Moses told the words of the people unto the Lord.

The Book of Numbers

Numbers 14:11
And the Lord said unto Moses, How long will this people provoke me? and how long will it be ere they **believe** me, for all the signs which I have shewed among them?

Numbers 12:7
My servant Moses is not so, who is **faithful** in all mine house.

Numbers 20:12
And the Lord spake unto Moses and Aaron, Because ye **believed** me not, to sanctify me in the eyes of the children of Israel, therefore ye shall not bring this congregation into the land which I have given them.

The Book of Deuteronomy

Deuteronomy 9:23

Likewise when the Lord sent you from Kadeshbarnea, saying, Go up and possess the land which I have given you; then ye rebelled against the commandment of the Lord your God, and ye **believed** him not, nor hearkened to his voice.

Deuteronomy 32:20

And he said, I will hide my face from them, I will see what their end shall be: for they are a very froward generation, children in whom is no **faith**.

The Book of 1 Samuel

1 Samuel 2:35
And I will raise me up a **faithful** priest, that shall do according to that which is in mine heart and in my mind: and I will build him a sure house; and he shall walk before mine anointed for ever.

The Book of 2 Chronicles

2 Chronicles 20:20
And they rose early in the morning, and went forth into the wilderness of Tekoa: and as they went forth, Jehoshaphat stood and said, Hear me, O Judah, and ye inhabitants of Jerusalem; **Believe** in the Lord your God, so shall ye be established; **believe** his prophets, so shall ye prosper.

The Book Of Nehemiah

Nehemiah 7:2
That I gave my brother Hanani, and Hananiah the ruler of the palace, charge over Jerusalem: for he was a **faithful** man, and feared God above many.

Nehemiah 9:8
And foundest his heart **faithful** before thee, and madest a covenant with him to give the land of the Canaanites, the Hittites, the Amorites, and the Perizzites, and the Jebusites, and the Girgashites, to give it, I say, to his seed, and hast performed thy words; for thou art righteous:

Nehemiah 13:13
And I made treasurers over the treasuries, Shelemiah the priest, and Zadok the scribe, and of the Levites, Pedaiah: and next to them was Hanan the son of Zaccur, the son of Mattaniah: for they were counted **faithful**, and their office was to distribute unto their brethren.

The Book of Psalm

Psalm 5:9
For there is no **faithfulness** in their mouth; their inward part is very wickedness; their throat is an open sepulchre; they flatter with their tongue.

Psalm 12:1
Help, Lord; for the godly man ceaseth; for the **faithful** fail from among the children of men.

Psalm 27:14
Wait on the Lord: be of good courage, and he shall strengthen thine heart: **wait**, I say, on the Lord.

Psalm 27:13
I had fainted, unless I had **believed** to see the goodness of the Lord in the land of the living.

Psalm 31:23
O love the Lord, all ye his saints: for the Lord preserveth the **faithful**, and plentifully rewardeth the proud doer.

Psalm 78:21-22

Therefore the Lord heard this, and was wroth: so a fire was kindled against Jacob, and anger also came up against Israel;
Because they **believed** not in God, and **trusted** not in his salvation:

Psalm 37:7

Rest in the Lord, and **wait** patiently for him: fret not thyself because of him who prospereth in his way, because of the man who bringeth wicked devices to pass.

Psalm 40:1

I **waited** patiently for the Lord; and he inclined unto me, and heard my cry.

Psalm 78:31-33

The wrath of God came upon them, and slew the fattest of them, and smote down the chosen men of Israel.
For all this they sinned still, and **believed** not for his wondrous works.
Therefore their days did he consume in vanity, and their years in trouble.

Psalm 101:6
Mine eyes shall be upon the **faithful** of the land, that they may dwell with me: he that walketh in a perfect way, he shall serve me.

Psalm 106:24
Yea, they despised the pleasant land, they **believed not** his word:

Psalm 116:10
I **believed**, therefore have I spoken: I was greatly afflicted:

Psalm 123:2
Behold, as the eyes of servants look unto the hand of their masters, and as the eyes of a maiden unto the hand of her mistress; so our eyes **wait** upon the Lord our God, until that he have mercy upon us.

The Book of Proverbs

Proverbs 13:17
A wicked messenger falleth into mischief: but a **faithful** ambassador is health.

Proverbs 14:5
A **faithful** witness will not lie: but a false witness will utter lies.

Proverbs 20:6
Most men will proclaim every one his own goodness: but a **faithful** man who can find?

Proverbs 25:13
As the cold of snow in the time of harvest, so is a **faithful** messenger to them that send him: for he refresheth the soul of his masters.

Proverbs 28:20
A **faithful** man shall abound with blessings: but he that maketh haste to be rich shall not be innocent.

The Book of Isaiah

Isaiah 28:16
Therefore thus saith the Lord God, Behold, I lay in Zion for a foundation a stone, a tried stone, a precious corner stone, a sure foundation: he that **believeth** shall not make haste.

Isaiah 40:31
But they that **wait** upon the Lord shall renew their strength; they shall mount up with wings as eagles; they shall run, and not be weary; and they shall walk, and not faint.

Isaiah 53:1
Who hath **believed** our report? and to whom is the arm of the Lord revealed?

Isaiah 64:4
For since the beginning of the world men have not heard, nor perceived by the ear, neither hath the eye seen, O God, beside thee, what he hath prepared for him that **waiteth** for him.

The Book of Daniel

Daniel 6:23

Then was the king exceedingly glad for him, and commanded that they should take Daniel up out of the den. So Daniel was taken up out of the den, and no manner of hurt was found upon him, because he **believe**d in his God.

The Book of Jonah

Jonah 3:5

So the people of Nineveh **believe**d God, and proclaimed a fast, and put on sackcloth, from the greatest of them even to the least of them.

The Book of Habakkuk

Habakkuk 1:5

Behold ye among the heathen, and regard, and wonder marvelously: for I will work a work in your days which ye will not **believe**, though it be told you.

Habakkuk 2:3-4

For the vision is yet for an appointed time, but at the end it shall speak, and not lie: though it tarry, **wait** for it; because it **will** surely come, it **will** not tarry.

Behold, his soul which is lifted up is not upright in him: but the just shall live by his **faith**.

Look at the proud; his soul is not straight or right within him, but the [rigidly] *just and the* [uncompromisingly] *righteous man shall live by his* **faith** *and in his* **faithfulness**. *(AMPLIFIED)*

Look, the one whose desires are not upright will faint from exhaustion, but the person of integrity will live because of his **faithfulness**. *(NET)*

The Book of Matthew

Matthew 6:30
Wherefore, if God so clothe the grass of the field, which to day is, and to morrow is cast into the oven, shall he not much more clothe you, O ye of little **faith**?

Matthew 8:10
When Jesus heard it, he marvelled, and said to them that followed, Verily I say unto you, I have not found so great **faith**, no, not in Israel.

Matthew 8:13
And Jesus said unto the centurion, Go thy way; and as thou hast **believe**d, so be it done unto thee. And his servant was healed in the selfsame hour.

Matthew 8:26
And he saith unto them, Why are ye fearful, O ye of little **faith**? Then he arose, and rebuked the winds and the sea; and there was a great calm.

Matthew 9:2

And, behold, they brought to him a man sick of the palsy, lying on a bed: and Jesus seeing their **faith** said unto the sick of the palsy; Son, be of good cheer; thy sins be forgiven thee.

Matthew 9:22

But Jesus turned him about, and when he saw her, he said, Daughter, be of good comfort; thy **faith** hath made thee whole. And the woman was made whole from that hour.

Matthew 9:28-29

And when he was come into the house, the blind men came to him: and Jesus saith unto them, **Believe** ye that I am able to do this? They said unto him, Yea, Lord.
Then touched he their eyes, saying, According to your **faith** be it unto you.

Matthew 13:58

And he did not many mighty works there because of their **unbelief.**

Matthew 14:31

And immediately Jesus stretched forth his hand, and caught him, and said unto him, O thou of little **faith**, wherefore didst thou doubt?

Matthew 15:28

Then Jesus answered and said unto her, O woman, great is thy **faith**: be it unto thee even as thou wilt. And her daughter was made whole from that very hour.

Matthew 16:8

Which when Jesus perceived, he said unto them, O ye of little **faith**, why reason ye among yourselves, because ye have brought no bread?

Matthew 17:17

Then Jesus answered and said, O **faithless** and perverse generation, how long shall I be with you? how long shall I suffer you? bring him hither to me.

Matthew 17:19-21

Then came the disciples to Jesus apart, and said, Why could not we cast him out?

And Jesus said unto them, Because of your
unbelief: for verily I say unto you, If ye have
faith as a grain of mustard seed, ye shall say unto
this mountain, Remove hence to yonder place;
and it shall remove; and nothing shall be
impossible unto you.
Howbeit this kind goeth not out but by prayer
and fasting.

Matthew 19:26
But Jesus beheld them, and said unto them, With
men this is impossible; but with God all things
are **possible**.

Matthew 21:21
Jesus answered and said unto them, Verily I say
unto you, If ye have **faith**, and doubt not, ye
shall not only do this which is done to the fig
tree, but also if ye shall say unto this mountain,
Be thou removed, and be thou cast into the sea; it
shall be done.

Matthew 23:23

Woe unto you, scribes and Pharisees, hypocrites! for ye pay tithe of mint and anise and cummin, and have omitted the weightier matters of the law, judgment, mercy, and **faith**: these ought ye to have done, and not to leave the other undone.

Matthew 21:32

For John came unto you in the way of righteousness, and ye **believed** him not: but the publicans and the harlots **believed** him: and ye, when ye had seen it, repented not afterward, that ye might believe him.

Matthew 24:45

Who then is a **faithful** and wise servant, whom his lord hath made ruler over his household, to give them meat in due season?

Matthew 25:21

His lord said unto him, Well done, thou good and **faithful** servant: thou hast been **faithful** over a few things, I will make thee ruler over many things: enter thou into the joy of thy lord.

Matthew 25:23

His lord said unto him, Well done, good and **faithful** servant; thou hast been **faithful** over a few things, I will make thee ruler over many things: enter thou into the joy of thy lord.

The Book of Mark

Mark 2:5
When Jesus saw their **faith**, he said unto the sick of the palsy, Son, thy sins be forgiven thee.

Mark 4:40
And he said unto them, Why are ye so fearful? how is it that ye have no **faith**?

Mark 5:34
And he said unto her, Daughter, thy **faith** hath made thee whole; go in peace, and be whole of thy plague.

Mark 5:36
As soon as Jesus heard the word that was spoken, he saith unto the ruler of the synagogue, Be not afraid, only **believe**.

Mark 9:19
He answereth him, and saith, O **faithless** generation, how long shall I be with you? how long shall I suffer you? bring him unto me.

Mark 9:23-24

Jesus said unto him, If thou canst **believe**, all things are possible to him that **believeth**. And straightway the father of the child cried out, and said with tears, Lord, I **believe**; help thou mine unbelief.

Mark 10:27

And Jesus looking upon them saith, With men it is impossible, but not with God: for with God all things are **possible**.

Mark 10:52

And Jesus said unto him, Go thy way; thy **faith** hath made thee whole. And immediately he received his sight, and followed Jesus in the way.

Mark 11:22-24

And Jesus answering saith unto them, Have **faith** in God.

For verily I say unto you, That whosoever shall say unto this mountain, Be thou removed, and be thou cast into the sea; and shall not doubt in his heart, but shall believe that those things which he saith shall come to pass; he shall have whatsoever he saith.

Therefore I say unto you, What things soever ye desire, when ye pray, **believe** that ye receive them, and ye shall have them.

Mark 16:11
And they, when they had heard that he was alive, and had been seen of her, **believed not**.

Mark 16:16-18
He that **believeth** and is baptized shall be saved; but he that **believeth** not shall be damned.
And these signs shall follow them that **believe**; In my name shall they cast out devils; they shall speak with new tongues;
They shall take up serpents; and if they drink any deadly thing, it shall not hurt them; they shall lay hands on the sick, and they shall recover.

Mark 16:14
Afterward he appeared unto the eleven as they sat at meat, and upbraided them with their unbelief and hardness of heart, because they **believed not** them which had seen him after he was risen.

The Book of Luke

Luke 1:20

And, behold, thou shalt be dumb, and not able to speak, until the day that these things shall be performed, because thou **believest** not my words, which shall be fulfilled in their season.

Luke 1:37-38

For with God nothing shall be **impossible**. And Mary said, Behold the handmaid of the Lord; be it unto me according to thy word. And the angel departed from her.

Luke 1:45

And blessed is she that **believed**: for there shall be a performance of those things which were told her from the Lord.

Luke 8:12-13

Those by the way side are they that hear; then cometh the devil, and taketh away the word out of their hearts, lest they should **believe** and be saved.

They on the rock are they, which, when they hear, receive the word with joy; and these have no root, which for a while **believe**, and in time of temptation fall away.

Luke 5:20
And when he saw their **faith**, he said unto him, Man, thy sins are forgiven thee.

Luke 8:50
But when Jesus heard it, he answered him, saying, Fear not: **believe** only, and she shall be made whole.

Luke 24:25
Then he said unto them, O fools, and slow of heart to **believe** all that the prophets have spoken:

Luke 7:9
When Jesus heard these things, he marvelled at him, and turned him about, and said unto the people that followed him, I say unto you, I have not found so great **faith**, no, not in Israel.

Luke 7:50
And he said to the woman, Thy **faith** hath saved thee; go in peace.

Luke 8:25
And he said unto them, Where is your **faith**? And they being afraid wondered, saying one to another, What manner of man is this! for he commandeth even the winds and water, and they obey him.

Luke 8:48
And he said unto her, Daughter, be of good comfort: thy **faith** hath made thee whole; go in peace.

Luke 9:41
And Jesus answering said, O **faithless** and perverse generation, how long shall I be with you, and suffer you? Bring thy son hither.

Luke 12:28
If then God so clothe the grass, which is to day in the field, and to morrow is cast into the oven; how much more will he clothe you, O ye of little **faith**?

Luke 17:5-6
And the apostles said unto the Lord, Increase our **faith**.

And the Lord said, If ye had **faith** as a grain of mustard seed, ye might say unto this sycamine tree, Be thou plucked up by the root, and be thou planted in the sea; and it should obey you.

Luke 17:19
And he said unto him, Arise, go thy way: thy **faith** hath made thee whole.

Luke 18:8
I tell you that he will avenge them speedily. Nevertheless when the Son of man cometh, shall he find **faith** on the earth?

Luke 18:27
And he said, The things which are impossible with men are **possible** with God.

Luke 18:42
And Jesus said unto him, Receive thy sight: thy **faith** hath saved thee.

Luke 19:17
And he said unto him, Well, thou good servant: because thou hast been **faithful** in a very little, have thou authority over ten cities.

Luke 22:32

But I have prayed for thee, that thy **faith** fail not: and when thou art converted, strengthen thy brethren.

Luke 24:11

And their words seemed to them as idle tales, and they **believed them not**.

The Book of John

John 1:12
But as many as received him, to them gave he power to become the sons of God, even to them that **believe** on his name:

John 1:50
Jesus answered and said unto him, Because I said unto thee, I saw thee under the fig tree, **believest** thou? thou shalt see greater things than these.

John 3:12
If I have told you earthly things, and ye **believe** not, how shall ye **believe**, if I tell you of heavenly things?

John 3:15-16
That whosoever **believeth** in him should not perish, but have eternal life.
For God so loved the world, that he gave his only begotten Son, that whosoever **believeth** in him should not perish, but have everlasting life.

John 4:48
Then said Jesus unto him, Except ye see signs
and wonders, ye will not **believe**.

John 4:50
Jesus saith unto him, Go thy way; thy son liveth.
And the man **believed** the word that Jesus had
spoken unto him, and he went his way.

John 5:38
And ye have not his word abiding in you: for
whom he hath sent, him ye **believe** not.

John 5:44
How can ye **believe**, which receive honour one
of another, and seek not the honour that cometh
from God only?

John 6:29
Jesus answered and said unto them, This is the
work of God, that ye **believe** on him whom he
hath sent.

John 6:64

But there are some of you that **believe not**. For Jesus knew from the beginning who they were that **believed not**, and who should betray him.

John 10:25

Jesus answered them, I told you, and ye **believed not**: the works that I do in my Father's name, they bear witness of me.

John 12:37

But though he had done so many miracles before them, yet they **believed not** on him:

John 20:29

Jesus saith unto him, Thomas, because thou hast seen me, thou hast **believed**: blessed are they that have not seen, and yet have **believed**.

John 20:27

Then saith he to Thomas, Reach hither thy finger, and behold my hands; and reach hither thy hand, and thrust it into my side: and be not **faithless**, but **believing**.

The Book of Acts

Acts 3:16
And his name through **faith** in his name hath made this man strong, whom ye see and know: yea, the **faith** which is by him hath given him this perfect soundness in the presence of you all.

Acts 6:5
And the saying pleased the whole multitude: and they chose Stephen, a man full of **faith** and of the Holy Ghost, and Philip, and Prochorus, and Nicanor, and Timon, and Parmenas, and Nicolas a proselyte of Antioch:

Acts 6:7
And the word of God increased; and the number of the disciples multiplied in Jerusalem greatly; and a great company of the priests were obedient to the **faith**.

Acts 6:8
And Stephen, full of **faith** and power, did great wonders and miracles among the people.

Acts 11:24

For he was a good man, and full of the Holy Ghost and of **faith**: and much people was added unto the Lord.

Acts 13:8

But Elymas the sorcerer (for so is his name by interpretation) withstood them, seeking to turn away the deputy from the **faith**.

Acts 13:41

Behold, ye despisers, and wonder, and perish: for I work a work in your days, a work which ye shall in no wise **believe**, though a man declare it unto you.

Acts 14:8-10

And there sat a certain man at Lystra, impotent in his feet, being a cripple from his mother's womb, who never had walked:
The same heard Paul speak: who stedfastly beholding him, and perceiving that he had faith to be healed,
Said with a loud voice, Stand upright on thy feet. And he leaped and walked.

Acts 14:22
Confirming the souls of the disciples, and exhorting them to continue in the **faith**, and that we must through much tribulation enter into the kingdom of God.
·

Acts 14:27
And when they were come, and had gathered the church together, they rehearsed all that God had done with them, and how he had opened the door of **faith** unto the Gentiles.

Acts 15:9
And put no difference between us and them, purifying their hearts by **faith**.

Acts 16:5
And so were the churches established in the **faith**, and increased in number daily.

Acts 16:15
And when she was baptized, and her household, she besought us, saying, If ye have judged me to be **faithful** to the Lord, come into my house, and abide there. And she constrained us.

Acts 20:21

Testifying both to the Jews, and also to the Greeks, repentance toward God, and **faith** toward our Lord Jesus Christ.

Acts 24:24

And after certain days, when Felix came with his wife Drusilla, which was a Jewess, he sent for Paul, and heard him concerning the **faith** in Christ.

Acts 26:18

To open their eyes, and to turn them from darkness to light, and from the power of Satan unto God, that they may receive forgiveness of sins, and inheritance among them which are sanctified by **faith** that is in me.

The Book of Romans

Romans 1:5
By whom we have received grace and apostleship, for obedience to the **faith** among all nations, for his name:

Romans 1:8
First, I thank my God through Jesus Christ for you all, that your **faith** is spoken of throughout the whole world.

Romans 1:12
That is, that I may be comforted together with you by the mutual **faith** both of you and me.

Romans 1:17
For therein is the righteousness of God revealed from **faith** to **faith**: as it is written, The just shall live by **faith**.

Romans 3:3
For what if some did not believe? shall their unbelief make the **faith** of God without effect?

Romans 3:22

Even the righteousness of God which is by **faith** of Jesus Christ unto all and upon all them that believe: for there is no difference:

Romans 3:25

Whom God hath set forth to be a propitiation through **faith** in his blood, to declare his righteousness for the remission of sins that are past, through the forbearance of God;

[handwritten annotation: MAKE RIGHT w/ GOD]

Romans 3:27

Where is boasting then? It is excluded. By what law? of works? Nay: but by the law of **faith**.

Romans 3:28

Therefore we conclude that a man is justified by **faith** without the deeds of the law.

Romans 3:30

Seeing it is one God, which shall justify the circumcision by **faith**, and uncircumcision through **faith**.

Romans 3:31
Do we then make void the law through **faith**?
God forbid: yea, we establish the law.

Romans 4:5
But to him that worketh not, but believeth on
him that justifieth the ungodly, his **faith** is
counted for righteousness.

Romans 4:9
Cometh this blessedness then upon the
circumcision only, or upon the uncircumcision
also? for we say that **faith** was reckoned to
Abraham for righteousness.

Romans 4:11
And he received the sign of circumcision, a seal
of the righteousness of the **faith** which he had
yet being uncircumcised: that he might be the
father of all them that believe, though they be not
circumcised; that righteousness might be
imputed unto them also:

Romans 4:12

And the father of circumcision to them who are not of the circumcision only, but who also walk in the steps of that **faith** of our father Abraham, which he had being yet uncircumcised.

Romans 4:13-14

For the promise, that he should be the heir of the world, was not to Abraham, or to his seed, through the law, but through the righteousness of **faith**.
For if they which are of the law be heirs, **faith** is made void, and the promise made of none effect:

Romans 4:16

Therefore it is of **faith**, that it might be by grace; to the end the promise might be sure to all the seed; not to that only which is of the law, but to that also which is of the **faith** of Abraham; who is the father of us all,

Romans 4:18-19

Who against hope **believed** in hope, that he might become the father of many nations, according to that which was spoken, So shall thy seed be.

And being not weak in **faith**, he considered not his own body now dead, when he was about an hundred years old, neither yet the deadness of Sarah's womb:

Romans 4:20
He staggered not at the promise of God through unbelief; but was strong in **faith**, giving glory to God;

Romans 5:1-2
Therefore being justified by **faith**, we have peace with God through our Lord Jesus Christ:
By whom also we have access by **faith** into this grace wherein we stand, and rejoice in hope of the glory of God.

Romans 9:30
What shall we say then? That the Gentiles, which followed not after righteousness, have attained to righteousness, even the righteousness which is of **faith**.

Romans 9:32

Wherefore? Because they sought it not by **faith**, but as it were by the works of the law. For they stumbled at that stumblingstone;

Romans 10:8-9

But what saith it? The word is nigh thee, even in thy mouth, and in thy heart: that is, the word of **faith**, which we preach;
That if thou shalt confess with thy mouth the Lord Jesus, and shalt **believe** in thine heart that God hath raised him from the dead, thou shalt be saved.

Romans 10:13-15

For whosoever shall call upon the name of the Lord shall be saved.
How then shall they call on him in whom they have not **believed**? and how shall they **believe** in him of whom they have not heard? and how shall they hear without a preacher?
And how shall they preach, except they be sent? as it is written, How beautiful are the feet of them that preach the gospel of peace, and bring glad tidings of good things!

Romans 10:17

So then **faith** cometh by hearing, and hearing by the word of God.

Romans 11:20

Well; because of unbelief they were broken off, and thou standest by **faith**. Be not highminded, but fear:

Romans 12:3

For I say, through the grace given unto me, to every man that is among you, not to think of himself more highly than he ought to think; but to think soberly, according as God hath dealt to every man the measure of **faith**.

Romans 12:6

Having then gifts differing according to the grace that is given to us, whether prophecy, let us prophesy according to the proportion of **faith**;

Romans 14:1

Him that is weak in the **faith** receive ye, but not to doubtful disputations.

Romans 14:22
Hast thou **faith**? have it to thyself before God.
Happy is he that condemneth not himself in that
thing which he alloweth.

Romans 14:23
And he that doubteth is damned if he eat,
because he eateth not of **faith**: for whatsoever is
not of **faith** is sin.

Romans 16:26
But now is made manifest, and by the scriptures
of the prophets, according to the commandment
of the everlasting God, made known to all
nations for the obedience of **faith**:

The Book of 1 Corinthians

1 Corinthians 1:9
God is **faithful**, by whom ye were called unto the fellowship of his Son Jesus Christ our Lord.

1 Corinthians 2:5
That your **faith** should not stand in the wisdom of men, but in the power of God.

1 Corinthians 4:2
Moreover it is required in stewards, that a man be found **faithful**.

1 Corinthians 4:17
For this cause have I sent unto you Timotheus, who is my beloved son, and **faithful** in the Lord, who shall bring you into remembrance of my ways which be in Christ, as I teach every where in every church.

1 Corinthians 7:25
Now concerning virgins I have no commandment of the Lord: yet I give my judgment, as one that hath obtained mercy of the Lord to be **faithful**.

1 Corinthians 10:13

There hath no temptation taken you but such as is common to man: but God is **faithful**, who will not suffer you to be tempted above that ye are able; but will with the temptation also make a way to escape, that ye may be able to bear it.

1 Corinthians 12:9

To another **faith** by the same Spirit; to another the gifts of healing by the same Spirit;

1 Corinthians 13:2

And though I have the gift of prophecy, and understand all mysteries, and all knowledge; and though I have all **faith**, so that I could remove mountains, and have not charity, I am nothing.

1 Corinthians 13:13

And now abideth **faith**, hope, charity, these three; but the greatest of these is charity.

1 Corinthians 15:14

And if Christ be not risen, then is our preaching vain, and your **faith** is also vain.

1 Corinthians 15:17
And if Christ be not raised, your **faith** is vain; ye are yet in your sins.

1 Corinthians 16:13
Watch ye, stand fast in the **faith**, quit you like men, be strong.

The Book of 2 Corinthians

2 Corinthians 1:20
For all the **promises** of God in him are yea, and in him Amen, unto the glory of God by us.

2 Corinthians 1:24
Not for that we have dominion over your **faith**, but are helpers of your joy: for by **faith** ye stand.

2 Corinthians 4:13
We having the same spirit of **faith**, according as it is written, I believed, and therefore have I spoken; we also believe, and therefore speak;

2 Corinthians 5:7
(For we walk by **faith**, not by sight:)

2 Corinthians 8:7
Therefore, as ye abound in every thing, in **faith**, and utterance, and knowledge, and in all diligence, and in your love to us, see that ye abound in this grace also.

2 Corinthians 10:15

Not boasting of things without our measure, that is, of other men's labours; but having hope, when your **faith** is increased, that we shall be enlarged by you according to our rule abundantly,

2 Corinthians 13:5

Examine yourselves, whether ye be in the **faith**; prove your own selves. Know ye not your own selves, how that Jesus Christ is in you, except ye be reprobates?

The Book of Galatians

Galatians 1:23
But they had heard only, That he which persecuted us in times past now preacheth the **faith** which once he destroyed.

Galatians 2:16
Knowing that a man is not justified by the works of the law, but by the **faith** of Jesus Christ, even we have believed in Jesus Christ, that we might be justified by the **faith** of Christ, and not by the works of the law: for by the works of the law shall no flesh be justified.

Galatians 2:20
I am crucified with Christ: nevertheless I live; yet not I, but Christ liveth in me: and the life which I now live in the flesh I live by the **faith** of the Son of God, who loved me, and gave himself for me.

Galatians 3:2
This only would I learn of you, Received ye the Spirit by the works of the law, or by the hearing of **faith**?

Galatians 3:5

He therefore that ministereth to you the Spirit, and worketh miracles among you, doeth he it by the works of the law, or by the hearing of **faith**?

Galatians 3:7

Know ye therefore that they which are of **faith**, the same are the children of Abraham.

Galatians 3:8

And the scripture, foreseeing that God would justify the heathen through **faith**, preached before the gospel unto Abraham, saying, In thee shall all nations be blessed.

Galatians 3:9

So then they which be of **faith** are blessed with **faithful** Abraham.

Galatians 3:11

But that no man is justified by the law in the sight of God, it is evident: for, The just shall live by **faith**.

Galatians 3:12
And the law is not of **faith**: but, The man that doeth them shall live in them.

Galatians 3:14
That the blessing of Abraham might come on the Gentiles through Jesus Christ; that we might receive the promise of the Spirit through **faith**.

Galatians 3:22
But the scripture hath concluded all under sin, that the promise by **faith** of Jesus Christ might be given to them that believe.

Galatians 3:23
But before **faith** came, we were kept under the law, shut up unto the **faith** which should afterwards be revealed.

Galatians 3:24
Wherefore the law was our schoolmaster to bring us unto Christ, that we might be justified by **faith**.

Galatians 3:25

But after that **faith** is come, we are no longer under a schoolmaster.

Galatians 3:26

For ye are all the children of God by **faith** in Christ Jesus.

Galatians 5:5

For we through the Spirit wait for the hope of righteousness by **faith**.

Galatians 5:6

For in Jesus Christ neither circumcision availeth any thing, nor uncircumcision; but **faith** which worketh by love.

Galatians 5:22

But the fruit of the Spirit is love, joy, peace, longsuffering, gentleness, goodness, **faith**,

Galatians 6:10

As we have therefore opportunity, let us do good unto all men, especially unto them who are of the household of **faith**.

The Book of Ephesians

Ephesians 1:15
Wherefore I also, after I heard of your **faith** in the Lord Jesus, and love unto all the saints,

Ephesians 2:8
For by grace are ye saved through **faith**; and that not of yourselves: it is the gift of God:

Ephesians 3:12
In whom we have boldness and access with confidence by the **faith** of him.

Ephesians 3:17
That Christ may dwell in your hearts by **faith**; that ye, being rooted and grounded in love,

Ephesians 4:5
One Lord, one **faith**, one baptism,

Ephesians 4:13
Till we all come in the unity of the **faith**, and of the knowledge of the Son of God, unto a perfect man, unto the measure of the stature of the fulness of Christ:

Ephesians 6:16

Above all, taking the shield of **faith**, wherewith ye shall be able to quench all the fiery darts of the wicked.

The Book of Philippians

Philippians 1:25
And having this confidence, I know that I shall abide and continue with you all for your furtherance and joy of **faith**;

Philippians 1:27
Only let your conversation be as it becometh the gospel of Christ: that whether I come and see you, or else be absent, I may hear of your affairs, that ye stand fast in one spirit, with one mind striving together for the **faith** of the gospel;

Philippians 2:17
Yea, and if I be offered upon the sacrifice and service of your **faith**, I joy, and rejoice with you all.

Philippians 3:9
And be found in him, not having mine own righteousness, which is of the law, but that which is through the **faith** of Christ, the righteousness which is of God by **faith**:

The Book of Colossians

Colossians 1:2

To the saints and **faithful** brethren in Christ which are at Colosse: Grace be unto you, and peace, from God our Father and the Lord Jesus Christ.

Colossians 1:4

Since we heard of your **faith** in Christ Jesus, and of the love which ye have to all the saints,

Colossians 1:7

As ye also learned of Epaphras our dear fellowservant, who is for you a **faithful** minister of Christ;

Colossians 1:23

If ye continue in the **faith** grounded and settled, and be not moved away from the hope of the gospel, which ye have heard, and which was preached to every creature which is under heaven; whereof I Paul am made a minister;

Colossians 2:5

For though I be absent in the flesh, yet am I with you in the spirit, joying and beholding your order, and the stedfastness of your **faith** in Christ.

Colossians 2:7

Rooted and built up in him, and stablished in the **faith**, as ye have been taught, abounding therein with thanksgiving.

Colossians 2:12

Buried with him in baptism, wherein also ye are risen with him through the **faith** of the operation of God, who hath raised him from the dead.

Colossians 4:7

All my state shall Tychicus declare unto you, who is a beloved brother, and a **faithful** minister and fellowservant in the Lord:

Colossians 4:9

With Onesimus, a **faithful** and beloved brother, who is one of you. They shall make known unto you all things which are done here.

The Book of 1 Thessalonians

1 Thessalonians 1:3

Remembering without ceasing your work of **faith**, and labour of love, and patience of hope in our Lord Jesus Christ, in the sight of God and our Father;

1 Thessalonians 1:8

For from you sounded out the word of the Lord not only in Macedonia and Achaia, but also in every place your **faith** to God-ward is spread abroad; so that we need not to speak any thing.

1 Thessalonians 2:13

For this cause also thank we God without ceasing, because, when ye received the word of God which ye heard of us, ye received it not as the word of men, but as it is in truth, the word of God, which effectually worketh also in you that **believe**.

1 Thessalonians 3:2

And sent Timotheus, our brother, and minister of God, and our fellow labourer in the gospel of Christ, to establish you, and to comfort you concerning your **faith**:

1 Thessalonians 3:5

For this cause, when I could no longer forbear, I sent to know your **faith**, lest by some means the tempter have tempted you, and our labour be in vain.

1 Thessalonians 3:6

But now when Timotheus came from you unto us, and brought us good tidings of your **faith** and charity, and that ye have good remembrance of us always, desiring greatly to see us, as we also to see you:

1 Thessalonians 3:7

Therefore, brethren, we were comforted over you in all our affliction and distress by your **faith**:

1 Thessalonians 3:10

Night and day praying exceedingly that we might see your face, and might perfect that which is lacking in your **faith**?

1 Thessalonians 5:8

But let us, who are of the day, be sober, putting on the breastplate of **faith** and love; and for an helmet, the hope of salvation.

1 Thessalonians 5:24

Faithful is he that calleth you, who also will do it.

The Book of 2 Thessalonians

2 Thessalonians 1:3
We are bound to thank God always for you, brethren, as it is meet, because that your **faith** groweth exceedingly, and the charity of every one of you all toward each other aboundeth;

2 Thessalonians 1:4
So that we ourselves glory in you in the churches of God for your patience and **faith** in all your persecutions and tribulations that ye endure:

2 Thessalonians 1:11
Wherefore also we pray always for you, that our God would count you worthy of this calling, and fulfil all the good pleasure of his goodness, and the work of **faith** with power:

2 Thessalonians 3:2
And that we may be delivered from unreasonable and wicked men: for all men have not **faith**.

2 Thessalonians 3:3

But the Lord is **faithful**, who shall stablish you, and keep you from evil.

The Book of 1 Timothy

1 Timothy 1:2
Unto Timothy, my own son in the **faith**: Grace, mercy, and peace, from God our Father and Jesus Christ our Lord.

1 Timothy 1:4
Neither give heed to fables and endless genealogies, which minister questions, rather than godly edifying which is in **faith**: so do.

1 Timothy 1:5
Now the end of the commandment is charity out of a pure heart, and of a good conscience, and of **faith** unfeigned:

1 Timothy 1:12
And I thank Christ Jesus our Lord, who hath enabled me, for that he counted me **faithful**, putting me into the ministry;

1 Timothy 1:14
And the grace of our Lord was exceeding abundant with **faith** and love which is in Christ Jesus.

1 Timothy 1:19
Holding **faith**, and a good conscience; which some having put away concerning **faith** have made shipwreck:

1 Timothy 2:7
Whereunto I am ordained a preacher, and an apostle, (I speak the truth in Christ, and lie not;) a teacher of the Gentiles in **faith** and verity.

1 Timothy 2:15
Notwithstanding she shall be saved in childbearing, if they continue in **faith** and charity and holiness with sobriety.

1 Timothy 3:9
Holding the mystery of the **faith** in a pure conscience.

1 Timothy 3:13
For they that have used the office of a deacon well purchase to themselves a good degree, and great boldness in the **faith** which is in Christ Jesus.

1 Timothy 4:1
Now the Spirit speaketh expressly, that in the latter times some shall depart from the **faith**, giving heed to seducing spirits, and doctrines of devils;

1 Timothy 4:6
If thou put the brethren in remembrance of these things, thou shalt be a good minister of Jesus Christ, nourished up in the words of **faith** and of good doctrine, whereunto thou hast attained.

1 Timothy 4:12
Let no man despise thy youth; but be thou an example of the **believers**, in word, in conversation, in charity, in spirit, in **faith**, in purity.

1 Timothy 5:8
But if any provide not for his own, and specially for those of his own house, he hath denied the **faith**, and is worse than an infidel.

1 Timothy 5:12
Having damnation, because they have cast off their first **faith**.

1 Timothy 6:10

For the love of money is the root of all evil: which while some coveted after, they have erred from the **faith**, and pierced themselves through with many sorrows.

1 Timothy 6:11

But thou, O man of God, flee these things; and follow after righteousness, godliness, **faith**, love, patience, meekness.

1 Timothy 6:12

Fight the good fight of **faith**, lay hold on eternal life, whereunto thou art also called, and hast professed a good profession before many witnesses.

1 Timothy 6:21

Which some professing have erred concerning the **faith**. Grace be with thee. Amen.

The Book of 2 Timothy

2 Timothy 1:5
When I call to remembrance the unfeigned **faith** that is in thee, which dwelt first in thy grandmother Lois, and thy mother Eunice; and I am persuaded that in thee also.

2 Timothy 1:13
Hold fast the form of sound words, which thou hast heard of me, in **faith** and love which is in Christ Jesus.

2 Timothy 2:2
And the things that thou hast heard of me among many witnesses, the same commit thou to **faithful** men, who shall be able to teach others also.

2 Timothy 2:13
If we believe not, yet he abideth **faithful**: he cannot deny himself.

2 Timothy 2:18
Who concerning the truth have erred, saying that the resurrection is past already; and overthrow the **faith** of some.

2 Timothy 2:22
Flee also youthful lusts: but follow righteousness, **faith**, charity, peace, with them that call on the Lord out of a pure heart.

2 Timothy 3:8
Now as Jannes and Jambres withstood Moses, so do these also resist the truth: men of corrupt minds, reprobate concerning the **faith**.

2 Timothy 3:10
But thou hast fully known my doctrine, manner of life, purpose, **faith**, longsuffering, charity, patience,

2 Timothy 3:15
And that from a child thou hast known the holy scriptures, which are able to make thee wise unto salvation through **faith** which is in Christ Jesus.

The Book of Titus

Titus 1:9
Holding fast the **faithful** word as he hath been taught, that he may be able by sound doctrine both to exhort and to convince the gainsayers.

Titus 1:13
This witness is true. Wherefore rebuke them sharply, that they may be sound in the **faith**;

Titus 2:2
That the aged men be sober, grave, temperate, sound in **faith**, in charity, in patience.

Titus 1:1
Paul, a servant of God, and an apostle of Jesus Christ, according to the **faith** of God's elect, and the acknowledging of the truth which is after godliness;

Titus 1:4
To Titus, mine own son after the common **faith**: Grace, mercy, and peace, from God the Father and the Lord Jesus Christ our Saviour.

The Book of Philemon

Philemon 1:5

Hearing of thy love and **faith**, which thou hast toward the Lord Jesus, and toward all saints;

Philemon 1:6

That the communication of thy **faith** may become effectual by the acknowledging of every good thing which is in you in Christ Jesus.

The Book of Hebrews

Hebrews 3:12
Take heed, brethren, lest there be in any of you an evil heart of **unbelief**, in departing from the living God.

Hebrews 3:19
So we see that they could not enter in because of **unbelief**.

Hebrews 4:2-3
For unto us was the gospel preached, as well as unto them: but the word preached did not profit them, not being mixed with **faith** in them that heard it.
For we which have **believe**d do enter into rest, as he said, As I have sworn in my wrath, if they shall enter into my rest: although the works were finished from the foundation of the world.

Hebrews 4:11
Let us labour therefore to enter into that rest, lest any man fall after the same example of **unbelief**.

Hebrews 6:12

That ye be not slothful, but followers of them who through **faith** and patience inherit the promises.

Hebrews 10:22

Let us draw near with a true heart in full assurance of **faith**, having our hearts sprinkled from an evil conscience, and our bodies washed with pure water.

Hebrews 10:38-39

Now the just shall live by **faith**: but if any man draw back, my soul shall have no pleasure in him.
But we are not of them who draw back unto perdition; but of them that **believe** to the saving of the soul.

Hebrews 11:1

Now **faith** is the substance of things hoped for, the evidence of things not seen.

Hebrews 11:3

Through **faith** we understand that the worlds were framed by the word of God, so that things which are seen were not made of things which do appear.

Hebrews 11:4

By **faith** Abel offered unto God a more excellent sacrifice than Cain, by which he obtained witness that he was righteous, God testifying of his gifts: and by it he being dead yet speaketh.

Hebrews 11:5

By **faith** Enoch was translated that he should not see death; and was not found, because God had translated him: for before his translation he had this testimony, that he pleased God.

Hebrews 11:6

But without **faith** it is impossible to please him: for he that cometh to God must believe that he is, and that he is a rewarder of them that diligently seek him.

Hebrews 11:7
By **faith** Noah, being warned of God of things not seen as yet, moved with fear, prepared an ark to the saving of his house; by the which he condemned the world, and became heir of the righteousness which is by **faith**.

Hebrews 11:8
By **faith** Abraham, when he was called to go out into a place which he should after receive for an inheritance, obeyed; and he went out, not knowing whither he went.

Hebrews 11:9
By **faith** he sojourned in the land of promise, as in a strange country, dwelling in tabernacles with Isaac and Jacob, the heirs with him of the same promise:

Hebrews 11:11
Through **faith** also Sara herself received strength to conceive seed, and was delivered of a child when she was past age, because she judged him **faithful** who had promised.

Hebrews 11:13
These all died in **faith**, not having received the promises, but having seen them afar off, and were persuaded of them, and embraced them, and confessed that they were strangers and pilgrims on the earth.

Hebrews 11:17
By **faith** Abraham, when he was tried, offered up Isaac: and he that had received the promises offered up his only begotten son,

Hebrews 11:20
By **faith** Isaac blessed Jacob and Esau concerning things to come.

Hebrews 11:21
By **faith** Jacob, when he was a dying, blessed both the sons of Joseph; and worshipped, leaning upon the top of his staff.

Hebrews 11:22
By **faith** Joseph, when he died, made mention of the departing of the children of Israel; and gave commandment concerning his bones.

Hebrews 11:23
By **faith** Moses, when he was born, was hid three months of his parents, because they saw he was a proper child; and they were not afraid of the king's commandment.

Hebrews 11:24
By **faith** Moses, when he was come to years, refused to be called the son of Pharaoh's daughter;

Hebrews 11:27
By **faith** he forsook Egypt, not fearing the wrath of the king: for he endured, as seeing him who is invisible.

Hebrews 11:28
Through **faith** he kept the passover, and the sprinkling of blood, lest he that destroyed the firstborn should touch them.

Hebrews 11:29
By **faith** they passed through the Red sea as by dry land: which the Egyptians assaying to do were drowned.

Hebrews 11:30
By **faith** the walls of Jericho fell down, after they were compassed about seven days.

Hebrews 11:31
By **faith** the harlot Rahab perished not with them that believed not, when she had received the spies with peace.

Hebrews 11:33
Who through **faith** subdued kingdoms, wrought righteousness, obtained promises, stopped the mouths of lions.

Hebrews 11:39
And these all, having obtained a good report through **faith**, received not the promise:

Hebrews 12:2
Looking unto Jesus the author and finisher of ou **faith**; who for the joy that was set before him endured the cross, despising the shame, and is set down at the right hand of the throne of God.

Hebrews 13:7
Remember them which have the rule over you, who have spoken unto you the word of God: whose **faith** follow, considering the end of their conversation.

The Book of James

James 1:3
Knowing this, that the trying of your **faith** worketh patience.

James 1:6
But let him ask in **faith**, nothing wavering. For he that wavereth is like a wave of the sea driven with the wind and tossed.

James 2:1
My brethren, have not the **faith** of our Lord Jesus Christ, the Lord of glory, with respect of persons.

James 2:5
Hearken, my beloved brethren, Hath not God chosen the poor of this world rich in **faith**, and heirs of the kingdom which he hath promised to them that love him?

James 2:14
What doth it profit, my brethren, though a man say he hath **faith**, and have not works? can **faith** save him?

James 2:17
Even so **faith**, if it hath not works, is dead, being alone.

James 2:18
Yea, a man may say, Thou hast **faith**, and I have works: shew me thy **faith** without thy works, and I will shew thee my **faith** by my works.

James 2:20
But wilt thou know, O vain man, that **faith** without works is dead?

James 2:22-24
Seest thou how **faith** wrought with his works, and by works was **faith** made perfect?
And the scripture was fulfilled which saith, Abraham **believe**d God, and it was imputed unto him for righteousness: and he was called the Friend of God.
Ye see then how that by works a man is justified, and not by **faith** only.

James 2:26

For as the body without the spirit is dead, so **faith** without works is dead also.

James 5:15

And the prayer of **faith** shall save the sick, and the Lord shall raise him up; and if he have committed sins, they shall be forgiven him.

The Book of 1 Peter

1 Peter 1:5
Who are kept by the power of God through **faith** unto salvation ready to be revealed in the last time.

1 Peter 1:7
That the trial of your **faith**, being much more precious than of gold that perisheth, though it be tried with fire, might be found unto praise and honour and glory at the appearing of Jesus Christ:

1 Peter 1:9
Receiving the end of your **faith**, even the salvation of your souls.

1 Peter 1:21
Who by him do believe in God, that raised him up from the dead, and gave him glory; that your **faith** and hope might be in God.

1 Peter 4:19
Wherefore let them that suffer according to the will of God commit the keeping of their souls to him in well doing, as unto a **faithful** Creator.

1 Peter 5:9
Whom resist stedfast in the **faith**, knowing that the same afflictions are accomplished in your brethren that are in the world.

The Book of 2 Peter

2 Peter 1:1

Simon Peter, a servant and an apostle of Jesus Christ, to them that have obtained like precious **faith** with us through the righteousness of God and our Saviour Jesus Christ:

2 Peter 1:5

And beside this, giving all diligence, add to your **faith** virtue; and to virtue knowledge;

The Book of 1 John

1 John 5:4-5
For whatsoever is born of God overcometh the
world: and this is the victory that overcometh the
world, even our **faith**.
Who is he that overcometh the world, but he that
believeth that Jesus is the Son of God?

The Book of Jude

Jude 1:3
Beloved, when I gave all diligence to write unto
you of the common salvation, it was needful for
me to write unto you, and exhort you that ye
should earnestly contend for the **faith** which was
once delivered unto the saints.

Jude 1:20
But ye, beloved, building up yourselves on your
most holy **faith**, praying in the Holy Ghost,

The Book of Revelation

Revelation 2:19
I know thy works, and charity, and service, and **faith**, and thy patience, and thy works; and the last to be more than the first.

Revelation 13:10
He that leadeth into captivity shall go into captivity: he that killeth with the sword must be killed with the sword. Here is the patience and the **faith** of the saints.

Revelation 14:12
Here is the patience of the saints: here are they that keep the commandments of God, and the **faith** of Jesus.

Revelation 17:14
These shall make war with the Lamb, and the Lamb shall overcome them: for he is Lord of lords, and King of kings: and they that are with him are called, and chosen, and **faithful**.

John Eckhardt Ministries.com

Made in the USA
Charleston, SC
06 April 2016